Story by Elsie Nelley
Illustrations by Richard Hoit

Contents

Chapter 1

Saturday Morning

Sara lives on a farm in the country.
Last weekend, she stayed with her cousin, Angus.
He lives in the city.

On Saturday morning, Angus's mum
took Sara and Angus tenpin bowling.
This was the first time Sara and Angus
had been bowling.

The man who worked behind the desk
put their names into a computer.
"You're playing in Lane 12 today,"
he said. "Have fun!"

Chapter 2

The Big Screen

Angus's mum stopped to talk with some friends.

When Sara and Angus got to Lane 12,
Sara looked up and saw a large screen.
"Angus, why is that up there?" she asked.

"I don't know," Angus said. "It's not as big as the screen down at the sports stadium, but it looks the same. If it is the same, we'll see ourselves on television."

Sara was delighted.
"Are we really going to be on television?" she asked.

"We'll just have to wait and see," said Angus.
"The camera might not turn on
until we start our game."

12

Sara stood quite close to the screen and stared up at it.
"Angus!" she said. "Have you ever been on television?"

Angus thought for a moment.
"I can't remember if I have or not," he said.
"But I think there is a camera here somewhere.
That must be why the man behind the desk
put our names into the computer.
They'll come up on the screen when the camera turns on."

Chapter 3

Sara and the Camera

Sara frowned.
"I would like to know where the camera is hidden," she said.

"It must be up there somewhere," said Angus. "Go on, Sara, smile for the camera. Now, let's get the game started."

But Sara didn't smile for the camera. She just looked annoyed. "If someone had told me I was going to be on television, I would have picked something special to wear," she said.

Sara began to take off her jacket.

"What are you doing?" Angus asked. "It's cold in here."

"I don't want anyone to see me wearing this old jacket," Sara said. "My red top will look much better on television."

12

Sara was so excited!
She had always wanted to be a star on television.

“I wish I had a mirror so I could fix my hair,” she said. “Have you got a comb, Angus?”

“Sara!” he said. “We are here to play tenpin bowling. I’ll go first.”

“No! Wait a minute!” Sara whispered, looking around.
“I’m not ready yet. Where should I stand?
Do you think the camera might be on now?”

12

Chapter 4

Sara Gets Her Wish

When Angus's mum arrived at Lane 12,
Angus was getting ready to bowl,
and Sara was smiling up at the big screen.

"Sara, what are you doing?
It's not warm enough to take your jacket off,"
said Angus's mum. "Shouldn't you put it on again?"

"I will later," Sara replied.
"I think the camera is going to turn on soon."

Angus's mum was surprised.
"Camera? What camera?" she asked.

12

Then, Angus's mum looked up at the large screen.

"You two didn't think you were going to be on television, did you?" she asked. "There are no cameras up there. When your game starts, your names and your bowling scores go up on the screen."

Just then the screen lit up.

"Oh, no!" Sara said sadly.
"I really thought we were going to be on television."

1 2 3 4 5 6 7 8 9 10 Total
Angus
Sara
Mum
12

Angus's mum held up her phone.

"I'll take a video of you instead," she said, smiling. "Then you can be on our television at home!"